WELCOME T

Step into the enchanting world of Norway with this captivating history book tailored for middle school readers. Journey from the time of fierce Viking warriors and their legendary voyages, through the medieval unification of Norway under King Harald Fairhair, and into the periods of union with Denmark and Sweden. Witness Norway's path to independence, the struggles and triumphs during World War II, and its transformation into the modern, vibrant nation it is today.

Packed with engaging stories, fascinating facts, and colorful illustrations, this book brings Norway's rich history to life. Readers will explore the daily lives of Vikings, the political intrigues of medieval kings, the resilience of Norwegians during wartime, and the innovative spirit driving Norway's contemporary achievements.

Designed to spark curiosity and deepen understanding, this book makes history accessible and exciting. Each chapter is filled with vivid narratives and insightful details, perfect for young readers eager to learn. Discover the legends and legacy of Norway!

ILLUSTRATED WITH HISTORICAL PHOTOS

TABLE OF CONTENTS

INTRODUCTION	5
THE VIKING AGE	9
THE FORMATION OF THE KINGDOM	17
THE UNION PERIODS	27
ROAD TO INDEPENDENCE	35
20TH CENTURY NORWAY	43
MODERN NORWAY	51
TRADITIONAL FOODS	59
HISTORICAL & CULTURAL LOCATIONS	67
NORWEGIAN SPORTS	79
HISTORIC PEOPLE	89
REVIEW OF NORWAY'S HISTORY	99

PREIKESTOLEN CLIFF

INTRODUCTION

Welcome to Norway, a land of stunning fjords, majestic mountains, and a rich history. Imagine stepping into a time machine and traveling back to when fierce Viking warriors sailed the seas. In this book, you'll journey through Norway's past, from ancient times to the vibrant, modern country it is today.

Located in Northern Europe, Norway boasts breathtaking landscapes, with deep blue fjords, towering mountains, and endless forests. But Norway is more than its scenery; it's a country with a fascinating story to tell.

Our adventure begins with the Vikings, the seafaring warriors and traders who left their mark on Europe. You'll learn about their legendary raids, voyages to lands like Greenland, and their daily lives. Discover what they ate, how they built their famous longships, and the gods they worshipped.

Next, we'll explore the Middle Ages, a time of kings and kingdoms. You'll meet King Harald Fairhair, who united Norway into a single kingdom. Learn how life changed as Norway transitioned from rival chieftains to a unified nation.

We'll then move on to Norway's union periods. First, there was the Kalmar Union with Denmark and Sweden. Later, Norway came under Danish rule for nearly 400 years, shaping much of its culture and society. Finally, we'll cover the union with Sweden and Norway's eventual independence.

In the 19th century, Norway experienced a resurgence of national pride. In 1814, Norway adopted its own constitution and eventually achieved full independence in 1905. You'll read about the key figures and events that led to this.

The 20th century brought new challenges. During World War II, Norway was occupied by Nazi Germany. You'll learn about the resistance and how Norway emerged stronger after the war. The discovery of oil in the North Sea transformed Norway, leading to significant economic growth.

Today, Norway is known for its high standard of living, commitment to sustainability, and vibrant culture. From Oslo to the Lofoten Islands, Norway offers a unique blend of tradition and modernity. Discover how Norwegians celebrate their heritage and tackle global challenges.

As we journey through this book, you'll find stories of heroism, innovation, and resilience. Meet explorers, leaders, and everyday people who contributed to Norway's rich history. Let's dive in and discover the incredible story of Norway together.

Logan Stover

VIKING LONGSHIP

DAILY LIFE – VIKING VILLAGE

THE VIKING AGE

Our story begins in the mists of ancient Scandinavia, a time when Norway was a land of rugged landscapes and hardy people. Imagine the cold wind whipping through your hair as you stand on the deck of a Viking longship, the salt spray of the sea on your face. This is the world of the Vikings, the fierce warriors, and explorers who roamed the seas from the late 8th to the early 11th century.

The Vikings came from the Scandinavian countries of Norway, Denmark, and Sweden. They were skilled sailors and shipbuilders, known for their impressive longships that could navigate both open seas and shallow rivers. But the Vikings were more than just raiders; they were also traders, settlers, and farmers. At home in Norway, they lived in small communities along the fjords and valleys, farming the land and raising livestock.

The word "Viking" itself comes from the Old Norse word "vikingr," which means "pirate" or "raider." While many Vikings did embark on raids to far-off lands, seeking treasure and glory, others were peaceful traders who established settlements and traded goods such as furs, amber, and weapons.

Viking society was structured in a way that reflected their values of bravery, loyalty, and honor. At the top were the kings and jarls (noblemen), who ruled over territories and commanded warriors.

Below them were the karls, the free farmers and craftsmen who made up the bulk of the population. At the bottom were the thralls, or slaves, who were often captured during raids.

The Vikings worshipped a pantheon of gods and goddesses, each with their own domains and stories. Odin, the chief god, was associated with wisdom, war, and death. Thor, the god of thunder, was a protector of mankind, wielding his mighty hammer, Mjölnir. Freyja, the goddess of love and fertility, and Loki, the trickster god, also played important roles in Viking mythology.

The Vikings were renowned for their exploration and expansion. They traveled far beyond their homelands, reaching as far west as North America and as far east as the Caspian Sea. One of the most famous Viking explorers was Leif Erikson, who is believed to have reached the shores of North America around the year 1000, long before Christopher Columbus.

The Vikings also established settlements in places like Iceland, Greenland, and even parts of modern-day Russia and France. They founded the city of Dublin in Ireland and traded with the Byzantine Empire and the Islamic Caliphate. Their extensive network of trade routes and settlements helped to spread their influence and culture across Europe and beyond.

VIKING CHIEFTAIN CONDUCTING A CEREMONY

VIKING MARKET

Viking raids were both feared and legendary. Starting in 793 with the infamous raid on the monastery at Lindisfarne in England, Viking warriors launched swift and brutal attacks on coastal towns and villages across Europe. They used their longships to navigate rivers and attack inland targets, striking fear into the hearts of those they encountered.

Despite their reputation as ruthless raiders, the Vikings also had a complex and rich culture. They created beautiful art, crafted intricate jewelry, and wrote epic sagas and poems that have survived to this day. Their runic alphabet, used for writing inscriptions on stones and wood, provides a glimpse into their language and stories.

Life in Viking-age Norway was centered around the home and the family. Longhouses, made of wood and turf, were the typical dwellings. These large, communal buildings housed extended families and their animals, providing warmth and shelter during the harsh winters. Inside, a central hearth provided heat and light, and meals were cooked over an open fire.

Farming was a crucial part of Viking life. They grew crops such as barley, oats, and rye, and raised animals like cattle, sheep, and pigs. Fishing and hunting supplemented their diet, providing a source of protein and variety. Viking women played an important role in managing the household, spinning and weaving cloth, and preserving food for the winter months.

Viking children learned the skills they would need from an early age. Boys were taught to hunt, fish, and fight, while girls learned to manage the household and care for younger siblings. Both boys and girls were expected to contribute to the family's survival and success.

As we leave the Viking Age, remember that these seafaring warriors and traders laid the foundation for what would become the kingdom of Norway. Their legacy is still evident today, in the tales of their gods and heroes, the remnants of their settlements, and the enduring spirit of exploration and adventure that defines Norway.

Next, we'll explore the formation of the Norwegian kingdom and meet some of the powerful figures who shaped its early history. From the unification under King Harald Fairhair to the daily life of medieval Norwegians, there's much more to discover in the saga of Norway.

NORSE GODS ODIN, THOR, AND FREYA

KING HARALD FAIRHAIR

THE FORMATION OF THE KINGDOM

As the Viking Age drew to a close, Norway began to transform from a collection of scattered tribes and chieftains into a unified kingdom. This period of consolidation and nation-building was marked by fierce battles, strategic alliances, and the rise of legendary leaders.

Our story of unification starts with Harald Fairhair, the first king to rule over a united Norway. According to sagas, Harald vowed not to cut or comb his hair until he had united all of Norway under his rule. This earned him the nickname "Fairhair," as his locks grew long and flowing over the years.

Harald's quest for unification was driven by both ambition and love. The saga tells of his desire to marry Gyda, the daughter of a powerful chieftain, who refused his proposal unless he became the king of all Norway. Determined to win her hand, Harald embarked on a series of battles and conquests. He fought rival chieftains, forged alliances, and gradually brought the various regions of Norway under his control.

The Battle of Hafrsfjord, around 872 AD, was a decisive victory for Harald. This battle, fought in the fjords of southwestern Norway, marked the culmination of his efforts. After his victory, Harald declared himself the king of a united Norway. His reign laid the foundation for the kingdom, establishing a centralized authority that would shape the nation's future.

Harald Fairhair's unification was only the beginning. After his death, Norway faced periods of division and conflict as his descendants and other powerful families vied for control. The next significant figure in Norwegian history was King Olaf Tryggvason, who ruled from 995 to 1000 AD. Olaf was a formidable warrior and a devout Christian, and he played a crucial role in the Christianization of Norway.

Olaf Tryggvason's reign was marked by his efforts to convert the Norwegians from their traditional Norse paganism to Christianity. He built churches, baptized his subjects, and used both persuasion and force to spread the new faith. His influence was significant, and although he faced resistance, his efforts laid the groundwork for the eventual Christianization of Norway.

Following Olaf Tryggvason, another important figure emerged: King Olaf II Haraldsson, later known as Saint Olaf. Reigning from 1015 to 1028 AD, Olaf II continued the work of his predecessor, further solidifying Christianity in Norway. He is remembered for his efforts to create a more unified and organized kingdom, implementing new laws and governance structures. After his death in the Battle of Stiklestad in 1030, he was canonized as a saint, becoming a symbol of Norwegian identity and unity.

Medieval Norway was a land of contrasts, with rugged landscapes and tight-knit communities. Life was centered around the farmstead, which was the heart of social and economic activity. Families lived in longhouses, similar to those of the Viking Age, which provided warmth and shelter from the harsh climate.

Agriculture remained the backbone of the economy. Farmers grew crops such as barley, rye, and oats, and raised livestock, including cattle, sheep, and goats. The farming year was dictated by the seasons, with sowing in spring, tending crops in summer, and harvesting in autumn. During the long winter months, families would repair tools, spin and weave wool, and tell stories by the hearth.

Trade and craftsmanship also flourished during this period. Norwegian traders traveled along the coast and across the seas, exchanging goods such as fish, furs, and timber for luxury items like silk and spices. Craftsmen produced items from metal, wood, and textiles, contributing to the local economy and providing for the needs of their communities.

Religion played an increasingly important role in daily life. The spread of Christianity brought new traditions and practices. Churches became centers of worship and community gatherings, and religious festivals marked important times of the year. The old

DAILY LIFE IN EARLY MEDIEVAL NORWAY

VIKING ASSEMBLY

Norse gods gradually gave way to the Christian faith, which influenced art, literature, and societal values.

Education and learning began to take root, with monasteries and churches becoming centers of knowledge. Monks and priests copied manuscripts, preserving both religious texts and works of classical literature. The introduction of the Latin alphabet replaced the runic script, making written records more accessible and standardized.

As Norway's kingdom grew more stable, the rise of towns marked a significant development. Bergen, founded around 1070 by King Olaf III, became one of the most important trading centers in Northern Europe. Situated on the west coast, Bergen's natural harbor made it an ideal location for trade. It became a hub for the Hanseatic League, a powerful alliance of merchant guilds and market towns that dominated trade in the Baltic and North Seas.

Other towns, such as Trondheim and Oslo, also grew in importance. These urban centers became bustling markets where goods from across Europe were bought and sold. The growth of towns contributed to the development of a more complex society, with a growing class of merchants, artisans, and traders.

As we leave the formation of the kingdom behind, we can see how Norway transformed from a collection of warring chieftains to a unified kingdom.

The efforts of kings like Harald Fairhair and Olaf Tryggvason, the influence of Christianity, and the rise of towns and trade all played crucial roles in shaping medieval Norway. Our next chapter will take us through the union periods, where Norway's fate became intertwined with its Scandinavian neighbors, leading to centuries of political change and cultural development.

TRADITIONAL NORWEGIAN FEAST

MEDIEVAL NORWEGIAN CRAFTSMAN

SIGNING OF THE KALMAR UNION TREATY

THE UNION PERIODS

As the medieval period ended, Norway entered a new era marked by political unions with its Scandinavian neighbors. These unions brought both challenges and opportunities, shaping the nation's history in profound ways. The Kalmar Union and subsequent periods of Danish and Swedish rule left lasting imprints on Norway's culture, governance, and society.

The story of the Kalmar Union begins in 1397, when Queen Margrete I of Denmark successfully united Denmark, Norway, and Sweden under a single monarch. This political alliance, known as the Kalmar Union, was an attempt to consolidate power and protect the Scandinavian countries from external threats, particularly from the growing power of the German Hanseatic League and the Teutonic Knights.

Margrete I, a formidable and wise ruler, managed to bring the three kingdoms together by orchestrating the crowning of her great-nephew, Erik of Pomerania, as the king of the united realms. The union was intended to be a cooperative alliance, where each kingdom would retain its own laws and governance while sharing a common monarch and foreign policy.

However, the reality was more complex. While the union brought a period of relative peace and stability, it also faced internal conflicts and tensions.

The interests of Denmark often dominated the union, leading to discontent in Norway and Sweden. This dominance was partly due to Denmark's strategic location and stronger economy, which allowed it to exert more influence over the union's affairs.

The Kalmar Union eventually dissolved in the early 16th century, but Norway's close ties with Denmark continued. In 1536, after a series of conflicts and wars, Norway became an integral part of the Kingdom of Denmark-Norway. This union lasted for nearly 300 years, significantly impacting Norwegian society and culture.

During this period, Norway experienced both challenges and developments. Danish rule centralized political power in Copenhagen, Denmark's capital, reducing Norway's political autonomy. The Norwegian nobility, which had been relatively weak compared to other European countries, saw its influence wane further.

Despite these challenges, the union also brought positive changes. The Protestant Reformation, which began in the early 16th century, spread from Denmark to Norway, leading to significant religious and cultural shifts. The Lutheran Church replaced the Catholic Church as the state religion, and new educational institutions and printing presses emerged, promoting literacy and learning.

Norwegian society during this period remained

largely rural, with agriculture and fishing as the mainstays of the economy. However, the coastal towns continued to thrive as centers of trade and commerce. Bergen, in particular, maintained its position as a key trading hub, connecting Norway to the wider world.

The Napoleonic Wars in the early 19th century brought about significant geopolitical changes in Europe, including the dissolution of the Danish-Norwegian union. In 1814, following Denmark's defeat and the Treaty of Kiel, Norway was ceded to the King of Sweden. This marked the beginning of a new union, known as the Union between Sweden and Norway.

The transition was not smooth. Norwegians, eager to regain their independence, declared their own constitution and elected Prince Christian Frederick of Denmark as king in 1814. This brief period of independence, known as the Norwegian Constituent Assembly at Eidsvoll, lasted only a few months. The Swedish forces quickly moved to assert control, leading to the Convention of Moss, where Norway agreed to enter into a union with Sweden while retaining significant autonomy and its own constitution.

The Union between Sweden and Norway, which lasted from 1814 to 1905, was characterized by a delicate balance of power. Norway maintained its own parliament, legal system, and constitution, while

NORWEGIAN TOWN UNDER DANISH RULE

DANISH KING RULING OVER NORWAY

sharing a monarch and foreign policy with Sweden. This arrangement allowed for a degree of self-governance and national identity, even as Norway remained politically linked to Sweden.

Throughout these union periods, Norwegian culture and identity evolved in unique ways. The influence of Danish language and culture was particularly strong during the Danish rule. Danish became the language of the elite and administration, while Norwegian dialects persisted among the common people. This linguistic duality laid the groundwork for future language debates and the development of a distinct Norwegian written language.

Norwegian art, literature, and folklore also flourished, drawing inspiration from the country's rugged landscapes and Viking heritage. The Romantic Nationalism movement in the 19th century, which celebrated folk traditions, history, and nature, played a significant role in shaping Norwegian cultural identity. Artists like Johan Christian Dahl and writers like Henrik Wergeland and Asbjørnsen and Moe helped rekindle a sense of national pride and cultural uniqueness.

As the 19th century progressed, the desire for full independence grew stronger. Political movements advocating for greater autonomy and national sovereignty gained momentum. The Storting, Norway's parliament, played a crucial role in pushing for more control over domestic affairs.

The union with Sweden faced increasing strain, particularly over issues like foreign policy and the role of the monarchy. By the early 20th century, the drive for independence had become unstoppable. In 1905, Norway peacefully dissolved its union with Sweden, marking the beginning of a new era as a fully independent nation.

In the next chapter, we'll explore Norway's journey through the 20th century, including its experiences during World War II, its post-war recovery, and its emergence as a modern, prosperous country. From the challenges of occupation to the opportunities of economic growth, Norway's recent history is a testament to the resilience and determination of its people.

SIGNING OF THE NORWEGIAN CONSTITUTION AT EIDSVOLL IN 1814

ROAD TO INDEPENDENCE

The early 19th century was a tumultuous time for Norway, marked by shifting alliances, wars, and a growing sense of national identity. As we move through this chapter, we'll see how Norway transitioned from being a part of the Danish kingdom to achieving its own constitution and ultimately securing its independence from Sweden in 1905.

The Napoleonic Wars had far-reaching effects across Europe, including in Scandinavia. Denmark-Norway found itself on the losing side after aligning with Napoleon. In 1814, following Denmark's defeat, the Treaty of Kiel forced Denmark to cede Norway to the King of Sweden. This marked a significant turning point for Norway.

Norwegians, however, were not content to simply be transferred from one monarch to another. A surge of nationalistic fervor swept through the country. The Norwegian elite and influential leaders saw an opportunity to assert their independence. In the spring of 1814, prominent Norwegians gathered at Eidsvoll to draft a new constitution and establish an independent Norway.

The Constituent Assembly at Eidsvoll was a momentous event in Norwegian history. From April to May 1814, 112 representatives from across Norway convened to debate and draft a constitution. This document was inspired by the democratic ideals of the American and French revolutions, emphasizing individual freedoms, the rule of law, and popular sovereignty.

On May 17, 1814, the Norwegian Constitution was signed, establishing Norway as an independent kingdom. Prince Christian Frederick of Denmark was elected as the king of Norway. This day, now celebrated as Norway's National Day, marked the birth of a new nation built on democratic principles.

However, Norway's newfound independence was short-lived. Sweden, determined to assert its claim over Norway, launched a military campaign. Despite initial resistance, Norway was forced into a compromise. The Convention of Moss, signed in August 1814, allowed Norway to retain its constitution and a significant degree of autonomy, but it had to accept a union with Sweden under a common monarch.

The union with Sweden, lasting from 1814 to 1905, was characterized by a unique arrangement. Norway retained its own constitution, parliament (the Storting), and a high degree of self-governance. The two countries shared a monarch and coordinated their foreign policy, but day-to-day governance and internal affairs were managed independently.

Despite this arrangement, tensions between Norway and Sweden persisted. Norwegians were keen to assert their national identity and autonomy.

The union was often seen as an unequal partnership, with Swedish interests dominating key areas like foreign policy. These tensions fueled a growing movement for full independence.

Throughout the 19th century, Norway experienced significant social and economic changes. The Industrial Revolution brought about modernization, urbanization, and economic growth. A burgeoning middle class began to advocate for greater political representation and democratic reforms.

Key political figures emerged during this period, such as Johan Sverdrup, who championed parliamentary democracy and greater autonomy for Norway. The Storting (parliament) became a crucial platform for debating and advancing these ideas. By the late 19th century, the push for independence had become a central issue in Norwegian politics.

The tipping point came in the early 20th century, with disputes over the establishment of a separate Norwegian consular service. This issue highlighted the broader tensions within the union and Norway's desire for greater control over its international affairs. In 1905, these tensions reached a breaking point.

In 1905, the Norwegian Storting took decisive action. On June 7, it unilaterally declared the dissolution of the union with Sweden. This bold

NEGOTIATIONS BETWEEN NORWAY AND SWEDEN

CELEBRATING THE DISSOLUTION OF THE UNION WITH SWEDEN IN 1905

move was met with resistance from Sweden, but both nations were keen to avoid war. Intense negotiations followed, and a peaceful solution was reached.

A national referendum held in Norway overwhelmingly supported the dissolution of the union. On October 26, 1905, the dissolution was formally recognized, and Norway emerged as an independent nation. Prince Carl of Denmark was invited to become the new king of Norway, taking the name King Haakon VII.

With independence secured, Norway embarked on the challenging task of nation-building. The early 20th century was a time of optimism and growth. Norway focused on developing its infrastructure, economy, and cultural identity. The discovery of oil in the North Sea in the late 1960s would later transform the nation's economy, bringing unprecedented wealth and opportunities.

Norwegian culture flourished during this period, with a renewed interest in folk traditions, literature, and the arts. Figures like playwright Henrik Ibsen and painter Edvard Munch gained international recognition, contributing to Norway's cultural renaissance.

As we move into the 20th century, Norway faced new challenges and opportunities. The outbreak of World War II and the subsequent occupation by Nazi Germany tested the nation's resilience. Yet, Norway's recovery and post-war growth demonstrated the strength and determination of its people.

In the next chapter, we'll delve into Norway's experiences during World War II, its recovery and growth in the post-war era, and its emergence as a modern, prosperous country. From the courage of the resistance fighters to the prosperity brought by oil, Norway's recent history is a testament to the nation's enduring spirit and innovation.

NORWEGIAN RESISTANCE WORLD WAR II

20TH CENTURY NORWAY

The 20th century was a transformative period for Norway, marked by conflict, recovery, and remarkable economic growth. As we explore this chapter, we'll journey through Norway's experiences during World War II, its post-war recovery, and its emergence as a modern, prosperous nation.

In the early morning hours of April 9, 1940, the people of Norway awoke to the sounds of war. Nazi Germany had launched Operation Weserübung, an invasion of Denmark and Norway. Denmark quickly fell, but Norway, with its strategic importance for controlling the North Atlantic, resisted fiercely. The Norwegian government, along with the royal family, fled to the north and eventually went into exile in the United Kingdom.

Norwegian forces, along with British, French, and Polish troops, fought valiantly against the invaders. Despite their efforts, the Germans occupied Norway by June 1940. The occupation brought significant hardship and suffering. The Nazi regime imposed strict control, censored the press, and suppressed any form of resistance.

However, the spirit of resistance was strong among the Norwegian people. Underground groups, known collectively as the Norwegian Resistance, engaged in sabotage, espionage, and guerrilla warfare against the occupiers. They disrupted German supply lines, gathered intelligence for the Allies, and helped smuggle refugees, including Jews, to safety in Sweden.

One of the most famous acts of resistance was the sabotage of the heavy water plant at Vemork. The plant was crucial for the German atomic bomb project, and Norwegian saboteurs, in a daring operation, managed to destroy key parts of the facility, significantly delaying the Nazi nuclear program.

When World War II ended in 1945, Norway was left with the daunting task of rebuilding. The country had suffered significant damage, and the economy was in shambles. Nevertheless, the post-war years were marked by resilience, determination, and a spirit of cooperation.

Under the leadership of Prime Minister Einar Gerhardsen, known as "Landsfaderen" (Father of the Nation), Norway embarked on a comprehensive program of reconstruction and modernization. The government implemented social democratic policies that focused on welfare, education, and economic development. Key industries, such as shipping and fishing, were revitalized, and new infrastructure projects, including roads, schools, and hospitals, were undertaken.

Norway also became an active participant in international organizations. In 1949, it joined the

North Atlantic Treaty Organization (NATO), aligning itself with Western democracies in the face of the emerging Cold War. Norway played a crucial role in promoting peace and cooperation, and its diplomats were often involved in mediating international conflicts.

One of the most significant turning points in Norway's modern history came in the late 1960s with the discovery of oil in the North Sea. The Ekofisk oil field, discovered in 1969, marked the beginning of Norway's transformation into a major energy producer. The government established Statoil (now Equinor), a state-owned oil company, to manage and develop the nation's petroleum resources.

The oil boom brought unprecedented wealth to Norway. Revenue from oil exports funded extensive social programs, including healthcare, education, and pensions. The government also established the Government Pension Fund Global, commonly known as the "Oil Fund," to invest oil revenues for the benefit of future generations. Today, this fund is one of the largest sovereign wealth funds in the world.

The oil industry spurred technological innovation and economic diversification. Norwegian companies became leaders in offshore technology, developing expertise in deep-water drilling and environmental management. This technological prowess not only benefited the oil sector but also had spillover effects into other industries.

LIBERATION OF NORWAY IN 1945

POST-WAR REBUILDING EFFORTS

The second half of the 20th century saw significant social and cultural changes in Norway. The country experienced a wave of modernization, urbanization, and liberalization. Traditional rural lifestyles gave way to urban living, and cities like Oslo, Bergen, and Stavanger grew rapidly.

Norwegian society became more open and progressive. The feminist movement gained momentum, advocating for gender equality and women's rights. In 1981, Gro Harlem Brundtland became Norway's first female prime minister, symbolizing the progress made in gender equality. Her leadership on environmental issues also earned her international recognition.

The arts and culture flourished during this period. Norwegian literature, music, and cinema gained international acclaim. Writers like Knut Hamsun and Sigrid Undset, who won the Nobel Prize in Literature, and contemporary authors like Jo Nesbø and Karl Ove Knausgård brought Norwegian stories to a global audience. The music scene, from classical composer Edvard Grieg to modern bands like A-ha, showcased the diversity and creativity of Norwegian artists.

As we enter the 21st century, Norway stands as a prosperous and forward-looking nation. Its economy is robust, bolstered by the continued success of the oil and gas industry, as well as a strong focus on renewable energy and sustainability. Norway is a global leader in environmental policy, with ambitious goals to reduce carbon emissions and transition to a green economy.

Norwegian society is characterized by a high standard of living, excellent healthcare and education systems, and a strong social safety net. The country's commitment to equality, democracy, and human rights is reflected in its policies and international engagements.

Norway's natural beauty continues to be a source of pride and inspiration. The stunning fjords, mountains, and coastal landscapes attract tourists from around the world, while also serving as a reminder of the importance of preserving the environment.

In the next chapter, we'll delve into contemporary Norway, exploring its modern culture, technological advancements, and the challenges it faces in the 21st century. From innovative solutions to climate change to the celebration of cultural heritage, Norway's journey continues to be a story of resilience, innovation, and hope.

GEIRANGERFJORD

MODERN NORWAY

As we step into contemporary Norway, we find a nation that harmoniously blends tradition with modernity. The country has navigated the challenges of the 21st century with innovation, resilience, and a deep respect for its natural heritage. In this chapter, we will explore modern Norwegian culture, technological advancements, and the country's role in addressing global challenges.

Norway's economy remains robust, thanks largely to its rich natural resources. While oil and gas have historically been the backbone of the economy, Norway is making significant strides towards sustainability. The government has invested heavily in renewable energy sources, such as hydroelectric power, wind power, and even solar energy, despite its northern latitude.

The Government Pension Fund Global, or Oil Fund, continues to be a cornerstone of Norway's financial stability. This fund, worth over a trillion dollars, is invested globally and supports a wide range of public services, from healthcare to education. Importantly, the fund adheres to ethical guidelines, avoiding investments in companies that violate human rights or harm the environment.

Norway's commitment to sustainability extends beyond its borders. The country is a global leader in climate policy, aiming to become carbon-neutral by 2030. It has pioneered electric vehicle adoption, with EVs accounting for over half of all new car sales. This shift is supported by extensive charging infrastructure and incentives for EV owners.

Modern Norwegian culture is a vibrant blend of old and new. Traditional customs and contemporary practices coexist, creating a unique cultural landscape. The Sami people, indigenous to northern Norway, continue to practice their traditions, such as reindeer herding, while also participating fully in modern Norwegian society.

Norwegian literature, music, and art thrive on the global stage. Authors like Karl Ove Knausgård have gained international acclaim, while Norwegian music spans genres from black metal to electronic dance music. The Oslo Opera House and the Munch Museum are iconic cultural landmarks, attracting visitors from around the world.

The Norwegian lifestyle places a strong emphasis on outdoor activities and a connection to nature. Friluftsliv, or "open-air living," is a cherished concept that encourages spending time outdoors, whether hiking, skiing, or simply enjoying the natural surroundings. This love for nature is reflected in Norway's numerous national parks and protected areas.

Education and innovation are also pillars of

modern Norwegian society. The country boasts high literacy rates and a robust educational system. Universities and research institutions contribute to advancements in fields ranging from technology to environmental science. Norway's tech industry is growing, with startups and tech hubs emerging in cities like Oslo and Trondheim.

Like any country, Norway faces its share of challenges. Climate change poses a significant threat, with rising temperatures and changing weather patterns affecting the Arctic region and its ecosystems. The government is actively working on strategies to mitigate these impacts and promote sustainability.

Social issues, such as immigration and integration, are also important topics. Norway has welcomed refugees and immigrants, enriching its cultural tapestry but also requiring thoughtful policies to ensure successful integration. Efforts to combat discrimination and promote inclusivity are ongoing, reflecting Norway's commitment to human rights and equality.

Economic diversification is another priority. While the oil industry has been a major driver of prosperity, there is a growing focus on developing other sectors, such as technology, tourism, and renewable energy. This diversification aims to ensure long-term economic stability and reduce dependency on fossil fuels.

LOFOTEN

ÅLESUND

On the international stage, Norway is known for its commitment to peace and humanitarian efforts. The country has a long tradition of mediating conflicts and promoting human rights. Oslo has hosted numerous peace talks, including those for the Israeli-Palestinian conflict and the Colombian peace process.

Norway is also a major contributor to international development aid, supporting projects that address poverty, education, health, and climate change around the world. The Norwegian government and NGOs work in partnership with global organizations to improve living conditions in developing countries.

Norway's involvement in the Arctic Council underscores its strategic interest in the Arctic region. As climate change opens new shipping routes and access to resources, Norway advocates for sustainable development and cooperation among Arctic nations to protect this fragile environment.

Looking ahead, Norway is poised to continue its journey as a leader in sustainability, innovation, and social welfare. The nation's commitment to addressing global challenges, such as climate change and inequality, positions it as a model for other countries.

The younger generation of Norwegians is particularly engaged in shaping the future. Youth movements, such as the school strikes for climate inspired by Greta Thunberg, have a strong following in Norway. Young activists and entrepreneurs are driving forward initiatives in environmental protection, technology, and social justice.

Norway's emphasis on education, research, and innovation ensures that it remains at the forefront of global advancements. Initiatives to promote green technology, digital transformation, and sustainable living are integral to the nation's vision for the future.

As we conclude our journey through Norway's history, it's clear that the spirit of exploration, resilience, and innovation that defined the Vikings continues to shape he nation today. Norway's rich history, from the seafaring warriors of the past to the progressive society of the present, is a testament to the enduring strength and adaptability of its people.

Whether navigating the challenges of the medieval era, resisting occupation during World War II, or leading the way in sustainable development, Norway's story is one of continuous growth and transformation. As we look to the future, Norway stands as a beacon of hope and progress, a country that honors its heritage while boldly embracing the challenges and opportunities of tomorrow.

LUTEFISK

TRADITIONAL FOODS

No journey through Norwegian history and culture would be complete without a taste of its traditional foods. Norwegian cuisine is deeply rooted in the country's geography, climate, and history. From hearty stews to delicious pastries, the flavors of Norway offer a glimpse into the daily lives and traditions of its people. In this chapter, we will explore some of the most iconic Norwegian dishes and the stories behind them.

Norway's rugged landscape and long coastline have greatly influenced its cuisine. The country's cold climate and short growing season mean that preservation techniques, such as drying, smoking, and fermenting, have been essential for survival. Fish, particularly cod and salmon, have been staples in the Norwegian diet for centuries, while the forests and mountains provide game, berries, and mushrooms.

Fish and Seafood
Lutefisk: Perhaps one of the most famous (and sometimes infamous) traditional dishes, lutefisk is dried fish (usually cod) that has been soaked in a lye solution and then rehydrated. This process gives the fish a distinctive gelatinous texture. Lutefisk is typically served with boiled potatoes, peas, and a creamy mustard sauce, often during the Christmas season.

59

Rakfisk: This dish consists of fermented fish, usually trout. The fish is salted and stored in a cool place for several months to ferment. Rakfisk has a strong flavor and is often served thinly sliced with flatbread, sour cream, onions, and potatoes.

Gravlaks: A beloved delicacy, gravlaks is salmon that has been cured with a mixture of salt, sugar, and dill. It is traditionally served thinly sliced with mustard sauce and rye bread. Gravlaks originated as a method of preserving salmon and has become a staple at festive occasions and smorgasbords.

Klippfisk: Dried and salted cod, known as klippfisk, has been a significant part of Norwegian cuisine since the 17th century. Originally an export product, klippfisk is rehydrated and used in various dishes, including bacalao, a tomato-based stew with Portuguese influences.

Meat and Game
Pinnekjøtt: This traditional Christmas dish consists of salted and dried lamb ribs, which are steamed over birch branches and served with mashed rutabaga and potatoes. Pinnekjøtt is especially popular on the west coast of Norway.

Kjøttkaker: Norwegian meatballs, known as kjøttkaker, are made from ground beef mixed with flour, milk, and spices. They are typically served with boiled potatoes, gravy, and lingonberry sauce, making for a comforting and hearty meal.

Raspeballer: Also known as potato dumplings, raspeballer are made from grated potatoes mixed with flour and salt. They are often boiled and served with salted meat, sausage, or bacon, along with a side of mashed rutabaga and a generous helping of melted butter.

Elgstek: Roast elk (moose) is a popular dish in Norway, particularly in regions with abundant forests. The meat is marinated and slow-roasted, resulting in a tender and flavorful dish. It is commonly served with gravy, lingonberry sauce, and root vegetables.

Breads and Pastries
Flatbrød: This traditional Norwegian flatbread is made from barley or rye flour and is rolled thin and baked on a griddle. Flatbrød has a crisp texture and is often served with soups, stews, or as an accompaniment to meat and fish dishes.

Lefse: Lefse is a soft flatbread made from potatoes, flour, butter, and milk. It is typically rolled out thin and cooked on a griddle. Lefse can be enjoyed in various ways, such as spread with butter and sugar, wrapped around savory fillings, or served as a dessert with fruit and cream.

Kanelboller: Also known as cinnamon buns, kanelboller are sweet, spiced pastries that are popular

PINNEKJØTT

RØMMEGRØT

in Norway. They are made from a yeast dough, rolled with butter, sugar, and cinnamon, and baked until golden. Kanelboller are a favorite treat with a cup of coffee, enjoyed throughout the day.

Kransekake: This festive cake, often served at weddings, Christmas, and other celebrations, is made from almond flour, sugar, and egg whites. The dough is shaped into concentric rings and stacked to form a towering, cone-shaped cake. Kransekake is decorated with icing and sometimes filled with candies or small gifts.

Dairy and Desserts

Brunost: Brown cheese, or brunost, is a uniquely Norwegian cheese made from whey, cream, and milk. It has a caramel-like flavor and a smooth, fudge-like texture. Brunost is often sliced thin and served on bread or crispbread, sometimes accompanied by jam or honey.

Rømmegrøt: This traditional Norwegian porridge is made from sour cream, flour, and milk. Rømmegrøt is typically served with melted butter, sugar, and cinnamon, and is a popular dish during festive occasions and holidays.

Tilslørte Bondepiker: This delightful dessert, whose name translates to "veiled peasant girls," consists of layers of stewed apples, whipped cream, and toasted breadcrumbs. It is a simple yet delicious treat that showcases the natural sweetness of Norwegian apples.

Multekrem: A beloved Norwegian dessert, multekrem is made from cloudberries (multebær) and whipped cream. Cloudberries, which grow in the wild in northern Norway, have a unique tart flavor. Multekrem is often served with krumkake, a crisp, waffle-like cookie.

LOFOTEN ISLANDS

HISTORICAL & CULTURAL LOCATIONS

Norway is a land of stunning natural beauty and rich cultural heritage. From ancient Viking sites to modern architectural marvels, the country is dotted with historical and cultural landmarks that tell the story of its past and present. In this chapter, we will explore some of Norway's fascinating locations.

Viking Heritage Sites

Lofoten Islands: Located above the Arctic Circle, the Lofoten Islands are known for their dramatic scenery and deep-rooted Viking history. At the Lofotr Viking Museum in Borg, visitors can explore a reconstructed Viking longhouse, participate in traditional Viking activities, and learn about the daily life of the Vikings who lived here over a thousand years ago.

Stiklestad: Stiklestad is the site of the famous Battle of Stiklestad in 1030, where King Olaf II (later Saint Olaf) was killed. This battle was a turning point in Norway's history and played a crucial role in the country's Christianization. Today, the Stiklestad National Culture Centre hosts annual historical reenactments, educational programs, and cultural events to commemorate this significant event.

Gokstad and Oseberg Ship Burials: These burial sites, located near the town of Sandefjord, are home to some of the most well-preserved Viking ships ever discovered. The Gokstad and Oseberg ships, dating back to the 9th century, were found buried with a wealth of artifacts, offering invaluable insights into Viking burial customs and shipbuilding techniques. The ships are now housed in the Viking Ship Museum in Oslo.

Medieval and Religious Sites

Nidaros Cathedral: Located in Trondheim, Nidaros Cathedral is Norway's most important medieval building. Constructed over the tomb of Saint Olaf, it has been a site of pilgrimage for centuries. The cathedral is a stunning example of Gothic architecture, with intricate stone carvings, beautiful stained glass windows, and an impressive organ. It remains a central place of worship and a venue for important ceremonies.

Borgund Stave Church: One of the best-preserved stave churches in Norway, Borgund Stave Church dates back to the 12th century. This wooden church, located in the village of Borgund in Sogn og Fjordane, features intricate carvings and dragonhead details reminiscent of Viking art. Stave churches are unique to Norway and are a testament to the country's

NIDAROS CATHEDRAL

al craftsmanship and religious history.

Urnes Stave Church: Another remarkable stave church, Urnes Stave Church is a UNESCO World Heritage Site. Situated in Luster, overlooking the Sognefjord, it combines elements of Viking art with Romanesque architecture. The church's wooden carvings, depicting scenes from both pagan mythology and Christian iconography, are particularly noteworthy.

Castles and Fortresses

Akershus Fortress: Overlooking the Oslo Fjord, Akershus Fortress has stood guard over the capital city since the late 13th century. Built by King Haakon V to protect Oslo, the fortress has served various roles throughout history, including a royal residence, military base, and prison. Today, visitors can explore its medieval halls, dungeons, and museums, which offer insights into Norway's military history.

Bergenhus Fortress: Located in the heart of Bergen, Bergenhus Fortress is one of the oldest and best-preserved fortresses in Norway. It includes structures such as the Haakon's Hall, built in the 13th century, and the Rosenkrantz Tower, a fortified residence from the Renaissance period. The fortress grounds also host cultural events and concerts.

Modern Architectural Marvels

Oslo Opera House: A stunning example of modern architecture, the Oslo Opera House, located on the waterfront of Oslo, is designed to resemble an iceberg emerging from the water. Completed in 2008, it houses the Norwegian National Opera and Ballet. Visitors can walk on its sloping roof for panoramic views of the city and fjord, and enjoy performances in its state-of-the-art auditoriums.

The Norwegian National Museum: Set to open its new building in 2022, the National Museum in Oslo will be the largest art museum in the Nordic countries. It will house collections of traditional and contemporary art, design, and architecture, including works by famous Norwegian artists like Edvard Munch. The museum aims to be a vibrant cultural hub, showcasing Norway's rich artistic heritage.

The Arctic Cathedral: Located in Tromsø, the Arctic Cathedral (Tromsdalen Church) is an iconic modern church known for its striking triangular design, reminiscent of the Arctic landscape. Completed in 1965, it features a large stained glass window and impressive acoustics, making it a popular venue for concerts.

AKERSHUS FORTRESS

Cultural Landmarks and Museums

The Munch Museum: Dedicated to the life and work of the famous Norwegian painter Edvard Munch, the Munch Museum in Oslo houses an extensive collection of his art, including his most famous painting, "The Scream." The museum offers insights into Munch's artistic development and his impact on modern art.

The Vigeland Park: Also known as Frogner Park, this public park in Oslo is home to the world's largest sculpture park created by a single artist, Gustav Vigeland. The park features over 200 bronze and granite sculptures, including the iconic "Monolith" and "Angry Boy." Vigeland's sculptures explore themes of human life and relationships, making the park a unique cultural destination.

Bryggen in Bergen: A UNESCO World Heritage Site, Bryggen is a historic wharf in Bergen that dates back to the Hanseatic League's trading days. The colorful wooden buildings along the wharf are a testament to Bergen's rich mercantile history. Visitors can explore the narrow alleyways, museums, and shops that bring Bryggen's history to life.

Natural and Scenic Sites

Geirangerfjord: One of Norway's most famous fjords, Geirangerfjord is a UNESCO World Heritage Site known for its stunning natural beauty. The fjord is surrounded by steep mountains, cascading waterfalls, and lush vegetation. Visitors can take boat tours, hike scenic trails, and experience the breathtaking landscapes that define Norway's natural heritage.

North Cape (Nordkapp): Located on the island of Magerøya in northern Norway, North Cape is one of the northernmost points in Europe. Visitors can stand on the cliff's edge and gaze out over the Arctic Ocean, experiencing the midnight sun in summer and the polar night in winter. The North Cape Hall visitor center provides exhibits on the area's history and environment.

Exploring Norway's historical and cultural locations is like traveling through time, witnessing the evolution of a nation from its Viking roots to its modern achievements. Each site offers a unique story, reflecting the resilience, creativity, and spirit of the Norwegian people.

Whether you are walking through the ancient halls of Nidaros Cathedral, marveling at the modern design of the Oslo Opera House, or gazing at the

OSLO OPERA HOUSE

natural beauty of Geirangerfjord, these locations provide a deeper understanding of Norway's rich heritage and vibrant culture.

As you visit these landmarks, you will not only learn about Norway's past but also experience the enduring traditions and innovations that continue to shape this remarkable country. From historical sites that echo with the footsteps of kings and warriors to cultural hubs that celebrate art and nature, Norway invites you to discover its diverse and captivating story.

NORDKAPP

NORWEGIAN SKIING

NORWEGIAN SPORTS

Sports have played a significant role in Norwegian culture, reflecting the country's love for the outdoors, physical activity, and competitive spirit. From ancient Viking games to modern Olympic triumphs, the history of sports in Norway is a testament to the nation's dedication to excellence and the pursuit of athletic achievement. In this chapter, we will explore the development of various sports in Norway and celebrate some of its most memorable moments and athletes.

Ancient and Traditional Sports

Viking Games and Competitions: The Vikings were not only fierce warriors but also avid sports enthusiasts. They engaged in various physical activities to prepare for combat and demonstrate their strength and agility. Wrestling, known as "glíma," was a popular sport, along with stone lifting, archery, and horse racing. These games were not only forms of entertainment but also ways to build camaraderie and honor among the warriors.

Skiing: Skiing has a long and storied history in Norway, dating back over 4,000 years. Ancient rock carvings and historical records show that skiing was used for transportation, hunting, and military purposes. The word "ski" itself comes from the Old Norse word "skíð," meaning a split piece of wood. Skiing became a popular recreational activity in the 19th century, and Norway played a crucial role in developing modern skiing techniques and equipment.

Telemark Skiing: Named after the Telemark region in Norway, this style of skiing combines elements of alpine and Nordic skiing. It was developed in the mid-19th century by Sondre Norheim, considered the father of modern skiing. Telemark skiing features a distinctive turning technique and has influenced the evolution of skiing worldwide.

Winter Sports

Cross-Country Skiing: As one of the most iconic sports in Norway, cross-country skiing has deep roots in the country's culture. It became an organized sport in the late 19th century, with the first national championships held in 1909. Norway has produced many legendary cross-country skiers, including Bjørn Dæhlie and Marit Bjørgen, who have won numerous Olympic and World Championship medals.

Ski Jumping: Ski jumping is another beloved winter sport in Norway. The country is home to some of the

HOLMENKOLLEN SKI JUMP

most famous ski jumping hills, including Holmenkollen in Oslo, which hosts an annual World Cup event. Norwegian ski jumpers like Birger Ruud and Anders Jacobsen have achieved great success on the international stage.

Biathlon: Combining cross-country skiing and rifle shooting, biathlon is a demanding and exciting winter sport. Norway has a strong tradition in biathlon, with athletes like Ole Einar Bjørndalen, often referred to as the "King of Biathlon," who holds the record for the most Winter Olympic medals in biathlon.

Alpine Skiing: While not as dominant in alpine skiing as in Nordic disciplines, Norway has still produced world-class alpine skiers. Kjetil André Aamodt and Aksel Lund Svindal are among the country's most successful alpine skiers, winning multiple Olympic and World Championship medals.

Summer Sports

Football (Soccer): Football is one of the most popular sports in Norway, with a large following and numerous local clubs. The Norwegian national team has experienced periods of success, including qualifying for the FIFA World Cup in 1994 and 1998. Women's football is also highly popular, with the national team winning the FIFA Women's World Cup in 1995 and earning a reputation as one of the top teams globally.

Handball: Handball is another major sport in Norway, particularly in women's competitions. The Norwegian women's handball team has enjoyed significant success, winning multiple European Championships, World Championships, and Olympic medals. Players like Gro Hammerseng and Nora Mørk have become household names in Norway.

Track and Field: Norway has a proud tradition in athletics, producing several world-class athletes. Middle-distance runner Grete Waitz is one of the country's most celebrated athletes, having won nine New York City Marathons and a silver medal in the 1984 Olympic marathon. More recently, Jakob Ingebrigtsen has emerged as a star in middle-distance running, winning gold in the 1500 meters at the 2020 Tokyo Olympics.

Rowing: Rowing is another sport where Norway has excelled. The country has a strong tradition in rowing, with athletes like Olaf Tufte winning multiple Olympic medals. Norway's rowing clubs and beautiful waterways provide excellent conditions

NORWEGIAN SOCCER TEAM

for training and competition.

Modern Olympic Success

Winter Olympics: Norway has consistently been one of the top-performing nations in the Winter Olympics. The country's athletes have excelled in sports like cross-country skiing, biathlon, and ski jumping. Norway hosted the Winter Olympics twice: in Oslo in 1952 and in Lillehammer in 1994. The Lillehammer Games are often remembered as one of the best-organized Winter Olympics, showcasing Norway's passion for winter sports.

Summer Olympics: Although not as dominant in the Summer Olympics, Norway has achieved notable successes in sports like sailing, shooting, and athletics. The country's athletes have won medals in various disciplines, reflecting Norway's diverse sporting talent.

Outdoor Activities and Friluftsliv

The concept of "friluftsliv," or open-air living, is deeply ingrained in Norwegian culture. This philosophy encourages spending time outdoors and enjoying nature through activities like hiking, fishing, and skiing. Norway's vast wilderness areas, national parks, and scenic landscapes provide ample opportunities for outdoor sports and recreation, reinforcing the country's connection to nature.

The history of sports in Norway is a testament to the nation's love for physical activity, competition, and the great outdoors. From ancient Viking games to modern Olympic victories, sports have shaped Norway's cultural identity and brought its people together. Whether on the snowy slopes, the football field, or the running track, Norwegian athletes have demonstrated remarkable skill, determination, and sportsmanship.

As we celebrate Norway's sporting achievements and the values they represent, we are reminded of the importance of staying active, embracing challenges, and striving for excellence. The spirit of Norwegian sports continues to inspire future generations, fostering a sense of pride and unity that transcends the boundaries of time and place.

FRILUFTSLIV

OLAF TRYGGVASON

HISTORIC PEOPLE

Norway's history is rich with individuals who have left an indelible mark on the country's development and cultural heritage. From legendary Viking leaders to modern-day trailblazers, these figures have shaped Norway's identity and contributed to its legacy. In this chapter, we will explore the lives and achievements of some of the most influential and historic people in Norwegian history.

Viking Leaders

Harald Fairhair (c. 850–932): Often credited as the first king to unite Norway, Harald Fairhair's reign marked the beginning of a unified Norwegian kingdom. According to sagas, he vowed not to cut or comb his hair until he had consolidated his rule over all of Norway. Harald's efforts laid the foundation for the Norwegian state and its future kings.

Eric Bloodaxe (c. 895–954): The son of Harald Fairhair, Eric Bloodaxe was a fierce Viking warrior and king. His nickname, "Bloodaxe," reflects his reputation as a ruthless and formidable leader. Despite his short and tumultuous reign, Eric's legacy endures in the historical accounts of his exploits.

Leif Erikson (c. 970–1020): A renowned Viking explorer, Leif Erikson is often credited with being the first European to set foot in North America, around the year 1000. His journey to Vinland (believed to be present-day Newfoundland) predates Christopher Columbus's voyage by nearly 500 years. Leif's exploration opened new horizons for the Norse people and remains a significant chapter in the history of exploration.

Medieval Kings and Saints

Olaf Tryggvason (c. 960–1000): King of Norway from 995 to 1000, Olaf Tryggvason played a crucial role in the Christianization of Norway. He built churches, baptized his subjects, and used both persuasion and force to spread Christianity. Olaf's efforts significantly influenced Norway's religious and cultural development.

Saint Olaf (Olaf II Haraldsson) (995–1030): Also known as Saint Olaf, Olaf II Haraldsson was a king and later a canonized saint. His reign from 1015 to 1028 was marked by efforts to strengthen the central authority of the kingdom and promote Christianity. Olaf's death at the Battle of Stiklestad and subsequent canonization made him a national hero and a symbol of Norwegian unity and identity.

CHRISTIAN IV

Haakon IV Haakonsson (1204–1263): Haakon IV, also known as Haakon the Old, ruled during a period of relative peace and prosperity known as the Golden Age of the Norwegian medieval kingdom. He strengthened the monarchy, encouraged trade, and promoted cultural development. Haakon's reign saw the construction of significant buildings, including the Haakon's Hall in Bergen.

Renaissance and Early Modern Figures

Christian IV (1577–1648): Although he was a Danish king, Christian IV had a significant impact on Norway, which was part of the Danish-Norwegian union. He promoted economic development, built several towns, and supported the arts and education. Christian IV's legacy includes the founding of the city of Kristiansand in 1641.

Ludvig Holberg (1684–1754): Often regarded as the father of Danish-Norwegian literature, Ludvig Holberg was a prolific writer, historian, and playwright. His works, such as "Jeppe of the Hill" and "Niels Klim's Underground Travels," are celebrated for their wit, satire, and exploration of human nature. Holberg's contributions to literature and philosophy left a lasting impact on Scandinavian culture.

19th and Early 20th Century Figures

Henrik Ibsen (1828–1906): One of the most influential playwrights of all time, Henrik Ibsen is often referred to as the "father of modern drama." His works, including "A Doll's House," "Hedda Gabler," and "An Enemy of the People," challenged societal norms and explored themes of individualism, morality, and human psychology. Ibsen's plays continue to be performed and studied worldwide.

Edvard Grieg (1843–1907): A renowned composer and pianist, Edvard Grieg is celebrated for his contributions to Norwegian music and his role in the Romantic movement. His compositions, such as the "Peer Gynt" suites and "Piano Concerto in A minor," incorporate elements of Norwegian folk music and are beloved for their lyrical beauty and emotional depth.

Fridtjof Nansen (1861–1930): A polar explorer, scientist, diplomat, and humanitarian, Fridtjof Nansen is one of Norway's most remarkable figures. He led the first crossing of Greenland's interior and made significant contributions to Arctic exploration. Nansen's work with refugees and displaced persons earned him the Nobel Peace Prize in 1922.

HENRIK IBSEN

Roald Amundsen (1872–1928): A legendary polar explorer, Roald Amundsen is best known for being the first person to reach the South Pole in 1911. His achievements in polar exploration, including the first successful navigation of the Northwest Passage, solidified his reputation as one of the greatest explorers in history.

Modern Trailblazers

Thor Heyerdahl (1914–2002): An adventurer and ethnographer, Thor Heyerdahl gained international fame for his Kon-Tiki expedition in 1947, where he sailed a balsa wood raft from South America to the Polynesian islands to demonstrate the possibility of ancient transoceanic contact. His expeditions and theories sparked debates and brought attention to the study of early human migration.

Gro Harlem Brundtland (b. 1939): Norway's first female prime minister, Gro Harlem Brundtland served three terms and played a significant role in shaping modern Norwegian politics. She is also renowned for her work on sustainable development and public health, serving as the Director-General of the World Health Organization (WHO) and chairing the World Commission on Environment and Development, which made the Brundtland Report.

Jo Nesbø (b. 1960): A contemporary author known for his crime novels, Jo Nesbø has gained international acclaim for his gripping storytelling and complex characters. His series featuring detective Harry Hole has been translated into numerous languages and has captivated readers worldwide.

Marit Bjørgen (b. 1980): One of the greatest cross-country skiers of all time, Marit Bjørgen has won numerous Olympic and World Championship medals. Her dominance in the sport and her dedication to excellence have made her a national hero and an inspiration to athletes around the world.

THOR HEYERDAHL

MARIT BJØRGEN

REVIEW OF NORWAY'S HISTORY

As we reach the end of our exploration of Norway's rich and varied history, it's clear that this northern land is far more than its stunning fjords and majestic mountains. Norway's story is one of resilience, innovation, and a profound connection to both its natural environment and cultural heritage.

From the Viking Age to the Kingdom of Norway
Our journey began in the Viking Age, a time when fearless seafarers set sail from Norway's rugged shores, exploring and raiding far-off lands. The Vikings left an indelible mark on European history, with their tales of bravery, exploration, and fierce battles. This era laid the foundation for what would become the kingdom of Norway.

The unification under King Harald Fairhair marked the beginning of Norway as a unified entity. The medieval period brought further consolidation, the spread of Christianity, and the rise of towns and trade. Through the efforts of kings like Olaf Tryggvason and Saint Olaf, Norway forged a distinct national identity that would endure through centuries of change.

The Union Periods
The union periods, first under the Kalmar Union and later under Danish and Swedish rule, brought both challenges and opportunities. These centuries

99

were marked by struggles for autonomy, cultural integration, and economic development. Despite the dominance of foreign powers, Norway retained a strong sense of identity and tradition.

The early 19th century was a turning point. The 1814 Constitution, born out of a brief moment of independence, laid the groundwork for modern Norwegian democracy. The peaceful dissolution of the union with Sweden in 1905 was a testament to the country's determination and diplomatic skill. Norway emerged as a fully independent nation, ready to chart its own course.

The 20th Century

The 20th century was a time of profound transformation. Norway faced the horrors of World War II, endured occupation, and witnessed the bravery of its resistance fighters. The post-war years saw remarkable recovery, driven by social democratic policies, economic modernization, and international cooperation.

The discovery of oil in the North Sea in the late 1960s was a game-changer. It brought unprecedented wealth and allowed Norway to build a robust welfare state. The Government Pension Fund Global ensured that this wealth would benefit future generations, underpinning the country's prosperity and stability.

Contemporary Norway

Today, Norway is a beacon of innovation,

sustainability, and social progress. The country's commitment to renewable energy, environmental protection, and social welfare sets a global standard. Norway's role in international diplomacy and humanitarian efforts reflects its values of peace, cooperation, and human rights.

Modern Norwegian culture is a vibrant mix of tradition and modernity. From literature and art to music and outdoor living, Norwegians celebrate their heritage while embracing the future. The emphasis on education, research, and innovation ensures that Norway remains at the forefront of global advancements.

Looking to the Future

As Norway looks to the future, it faces both challenges and opportunities. Climate change, economic diversification, and social integration are key issues that will shape the coming decades. However, Norway's history of resilience and adaptability provides a strong foundation for addressing these challenges.

The younger generation, with their passion for sustainability, technology, and social justice, will play a crucial role in shaping Norway's future. Their engagement and innovation will continue the legacy of exploration and progress that has defined Norway for centuries.

BORGUND STAVE CHURCH

GLOSSARY

To help you understand some of the key terms and concepts mentioned throughout our journey in Norwegian history, here's a glossary of important terms:

Viking Age: The period from the late 8th century to the early 11th century, characterized by the Norse people's exploration, trade, and raids across Europe.

Longship: A type of ship used by the Vikings, known for its speed, agility, and ability to navigate both open seas and shallow rivers.

Kalmar Union: A political union of Denmark, Norway, and Sweden under a single monarch, established in 1397 and lasting until the early 16th century.

King Harald Fairhair: The first king to unify Norway, traditionally credited with founding the Norwegian kingdom in the late 9th century.

Olaf Tryggvason: A Norwegian king from 995 to 1000 AD, known for his efforts to Christianize Norway.

Saint Olaf (Olaf II Haraldsson): King of Norway from 1015 to 1028 AD, later canonized as a saint, known for consolidating the Christian faith in Norway and unifying the kingdom.

103

Constitution of 1814: The document signed at Eidsvoll on May 17, 1814, establishing Norway as an independent kingdom with a democratic constitution.

Treaty of Kiel: A treaty signed in 1814 that transferred Norway from Danish to Swedish control, following Denmark's defeat in the Napoleonic Wars.

Government Pension Fund Global (Oil Fund): A sovereign wealth fund established to invest revenues from Norway's petroleum industry for the benefit of future generations.

Friluftsliv: A Norwegian concept meaning "open-air living," emphasizing outdoor activities and a connection to nature.

Norwegian Resistance: The collective effort of underground groups in Norway to resist and sabotage the Nazi occupation during World War II.

Hydroelectric Power: A form of renewable energy generated by harnessing the power of flowing water, extensively used in Norway.

Equinor (formerly Statoil): A state-owned Norwegian oil and gas company, established to manage the country's petroleum resources.

Hanseatic League: A medieval commercial and defensive confederation of merchant guilds and market towns in Northwestern and Central Europe, with which Norwegian towns like Bergen had strong trading links.

Oslo Opera House: An iconic cultural landmark in Oslo, known for its striking architecture and cultural significance.

Sami People: Indigenous people of northern Norway, Sweden, Finland, and Russia, known for their unique culture, traditions, and reindeer herding.

NORWEGIAN FAMILIES − 1900

SOURCES & REFERENCES

Books

"The Almost Nearly Perfect People: Behind the Myth of the Scandinavian Utopia" by Michael Booth

"The History of Norway" by Karen Larsen

"The Vikings" by Neil Oliver

"Vikings: The North Atlantic Saga" edited by William W. Fitzhugh and Elisabeth I. Ward

"The Age of the Vikings" by Anders Winroth

"The Penguin History of the Vikings" by Gwyn Jones

"A History of Norway" by Knut Helle

"The Making of the Middle Ages in Norway" by Sverre Bagge

"The Norwegian-American Saga" by Odd S. Lovoll

"Norwegian Society, 1814-2014" edited by Knut Heidar and Einar Berntzen

"Nansen: The Explorer as Hero" by Roland Huntford

"Amundsen: The Greatest Polar Explorer" by Tor Bomann-Larsen

"Thor Heyerdahl and the Kon-Tiki Expedition" by Joe Steele

"Henrik Ibsen and the Birth of Modernism: Art, Theater, Philosophy" by Toril Moi

"Edvard Grieg: An Introduction to His Life and Music" by Einar Steen-Nøkleberg

Online Resources
Norwegian Directorate for Cultural Heritage (Riksantikvaren): https://www.riksantikvaren.no/

Norwegian National Archives (Arkivverket): https://www.arkivverket.no/

Norwegian Museum of Cultural History (Norsk Folkemuseum): https://norskfolkemuseum.no/

The Viking Ship Museum: https://www.khm.uio.no/english/visit-us/viking-ship-museum/

The Munch Museum: https://www.munchmuseet.no/en/

Norwegian Polar Institute: https://www.npolar.no/en/

The Official Site of Norway: https://www.visitnorway.com/

Norwegian Olympic and Paralympic Committee and Confederation of Sports: https://www.idrettsforbundet.no/

Museums and Cultural Institutions
Nidaros Cathedral: https://www.nidarosdomen.no/en/

Lofotr Viking Museum: https://www.lofotr.no/

Stiklestad National Culture Centre: https://www.stiklestad.no/

Borgund Stave Church: https://www.stavechurch.com/

Urnes Stave Church: https://www.visitnorway.com/listings/urnes-stave-church-(unesco)/18656/

Akershus Fortress: https://www.visitoslo.com/en/product/?tlp=1814735

Bergenhus Fortress: https://www.bergenhavn.no/bergenhus-festning

Academic Journals and Papers

Scandinavian Journal of History

The Journal of Norwegian Archaeology

Viking and Medieval Scandinavia

Norwegian Historical Review

Polar Record

Databases and Archives

Digital Archive of Norway: https://www.digitalarkivet.no/en/

National Library of Norway: https://www.nb.no/en/

UNESCO World Heritage Centre: https://whc.unesco.org/

Documentaries and Films

"Vikings Unearthed" (PBS)

"The Heavy Water War" (TV Mini-Series)

"Norway: A Time-Lapse Adventure"

"Kon-Tiki" (2012 Film)

"The Heroes of Telemark" (1965 Film)

Logan Stover is an Author, Historian, & Special Education Teacher from Southern California

"Logan makes learning fun!"

www.LoganStover.com

Explore Logan's Other Books
Amazon – eBay - Etsy

Printed in Great Britain
by Amazon